MW00891034

THIS BOOK BELONGS TO:

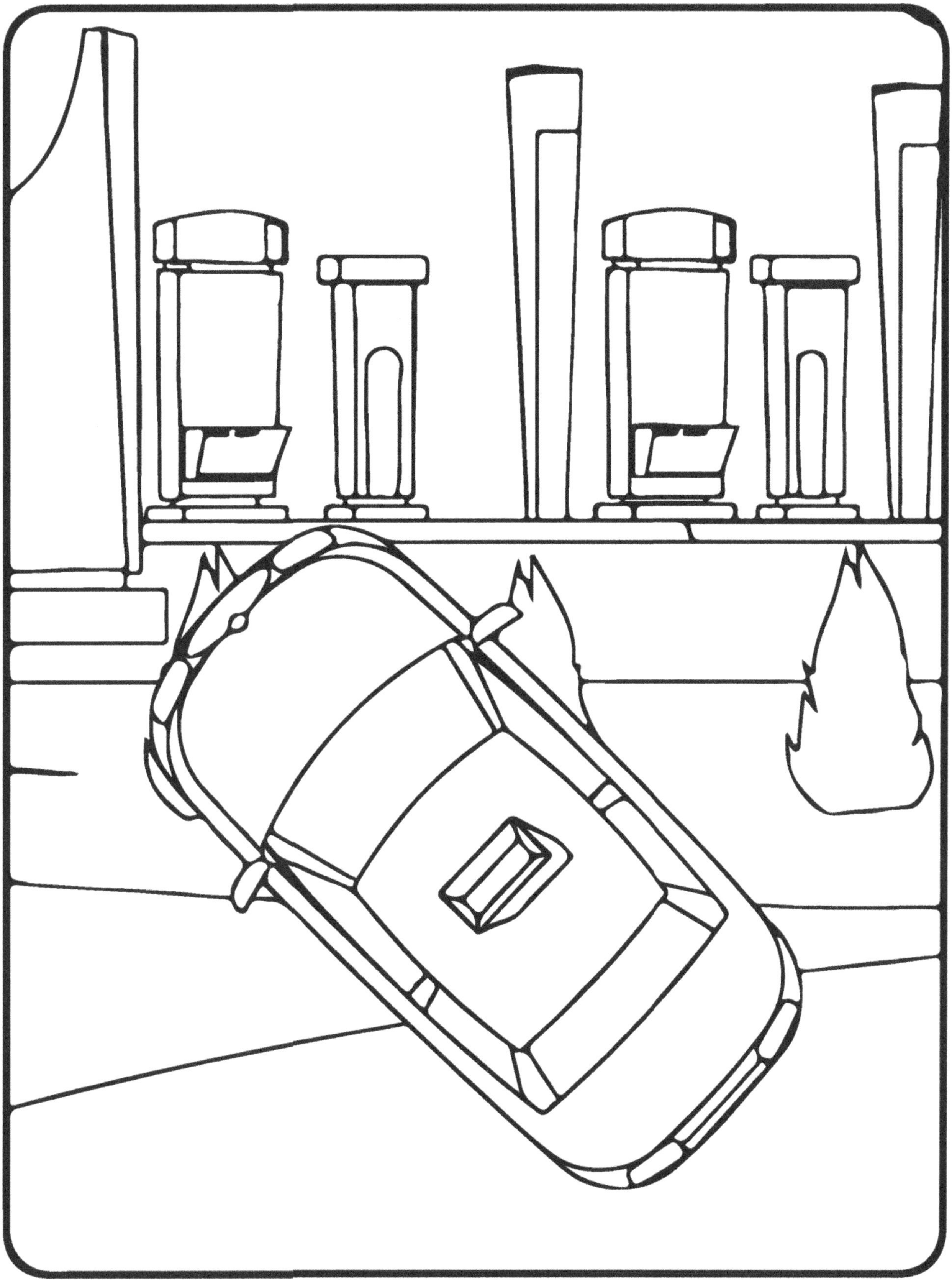

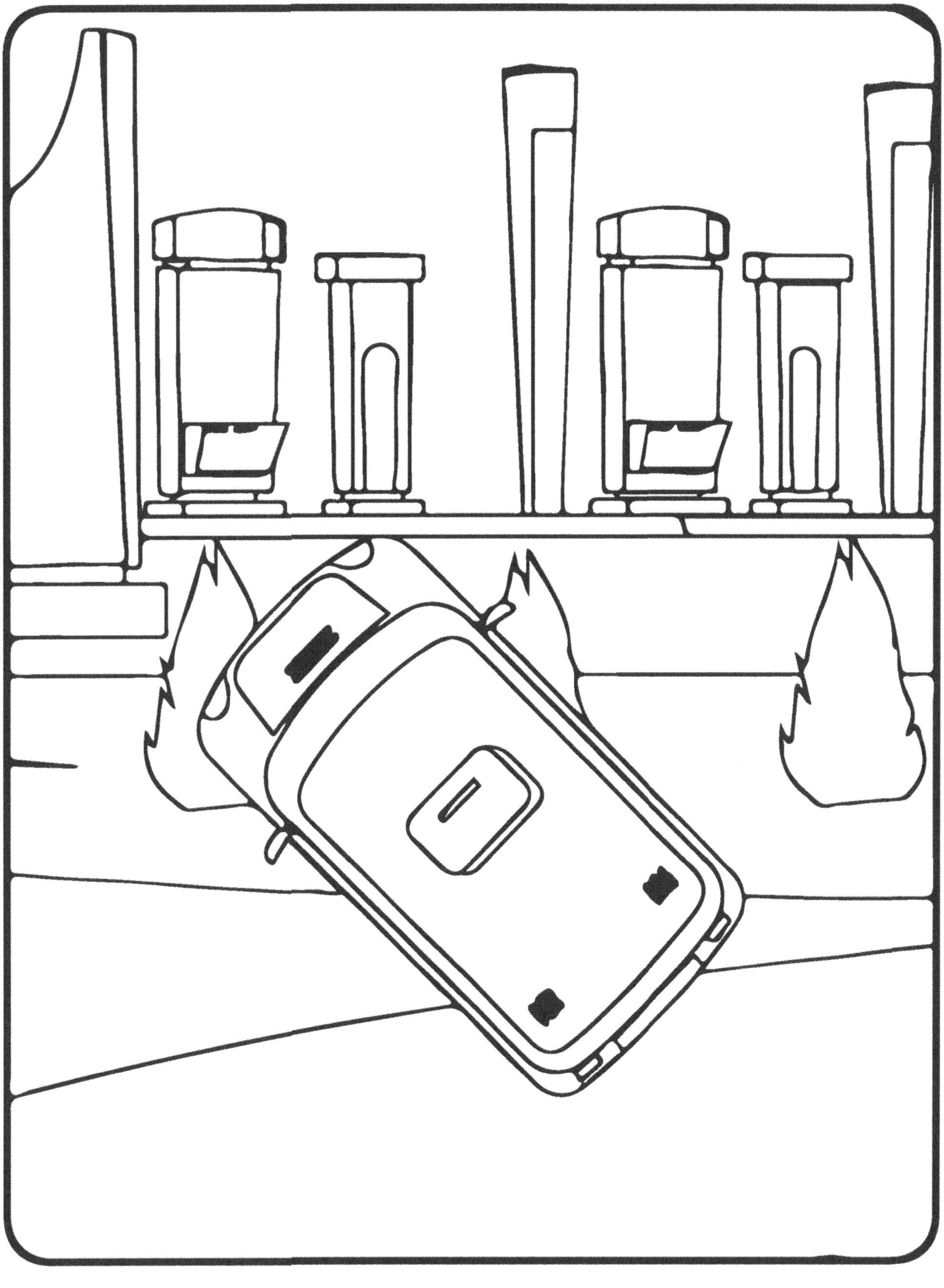

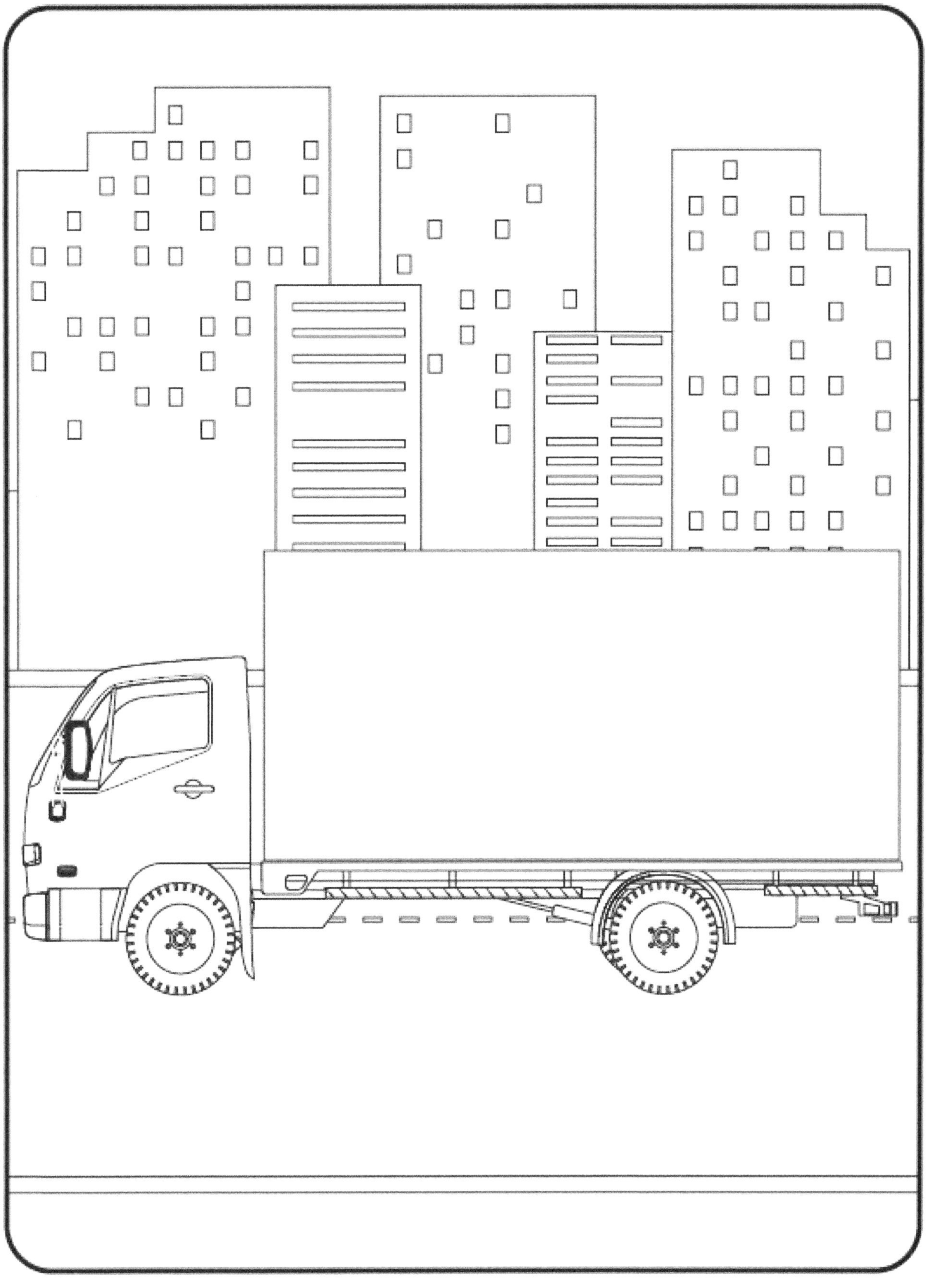

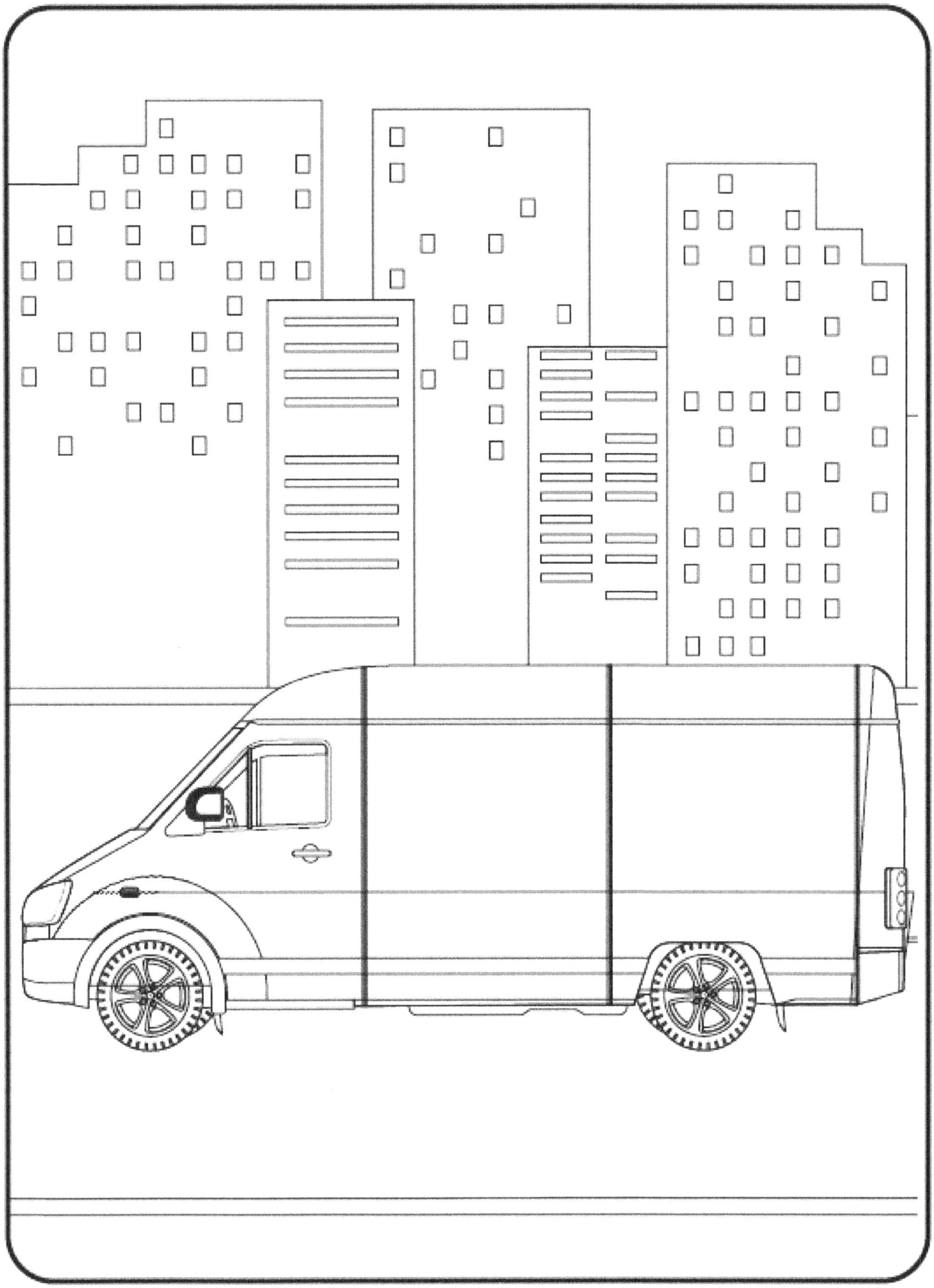

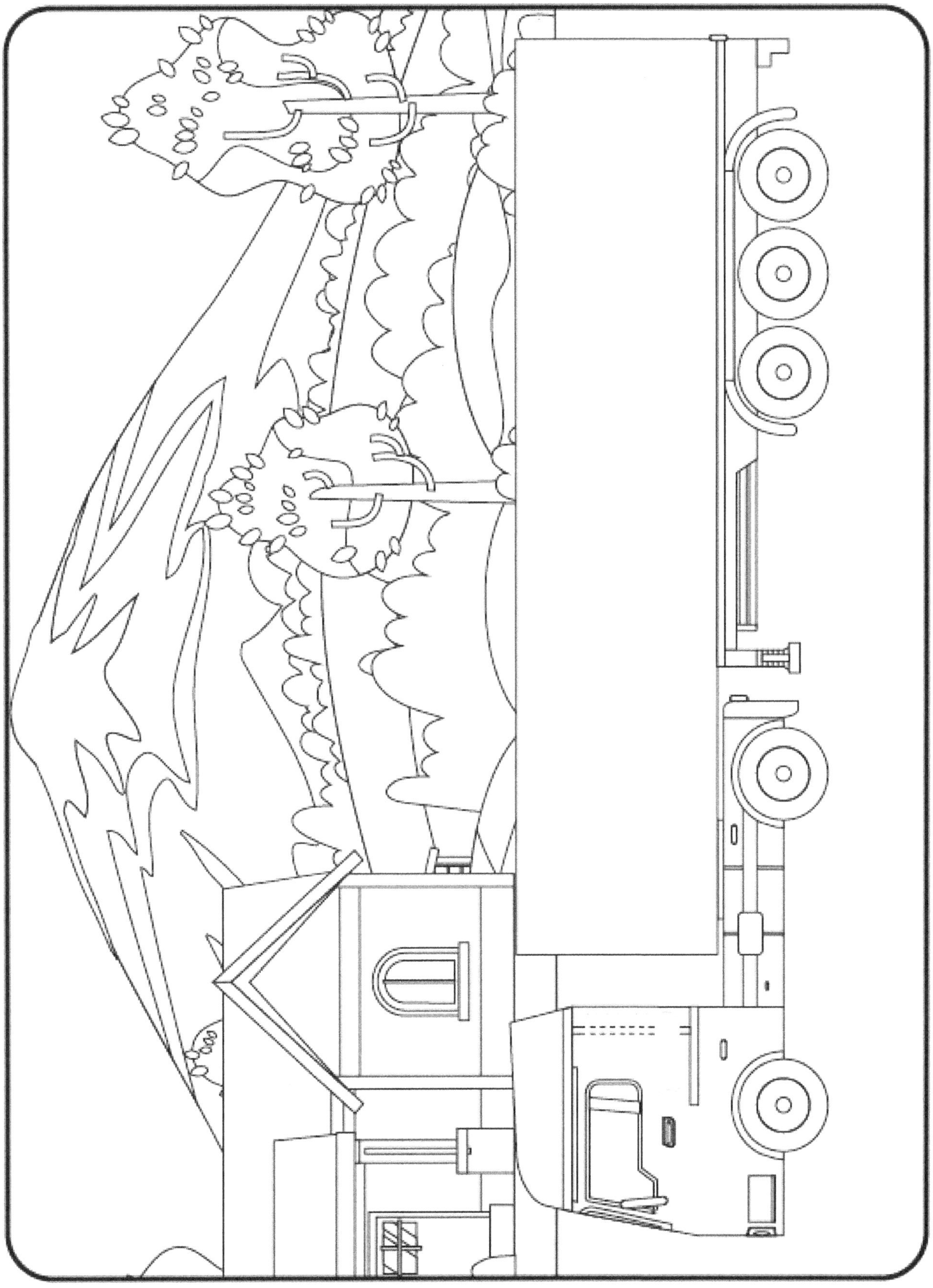

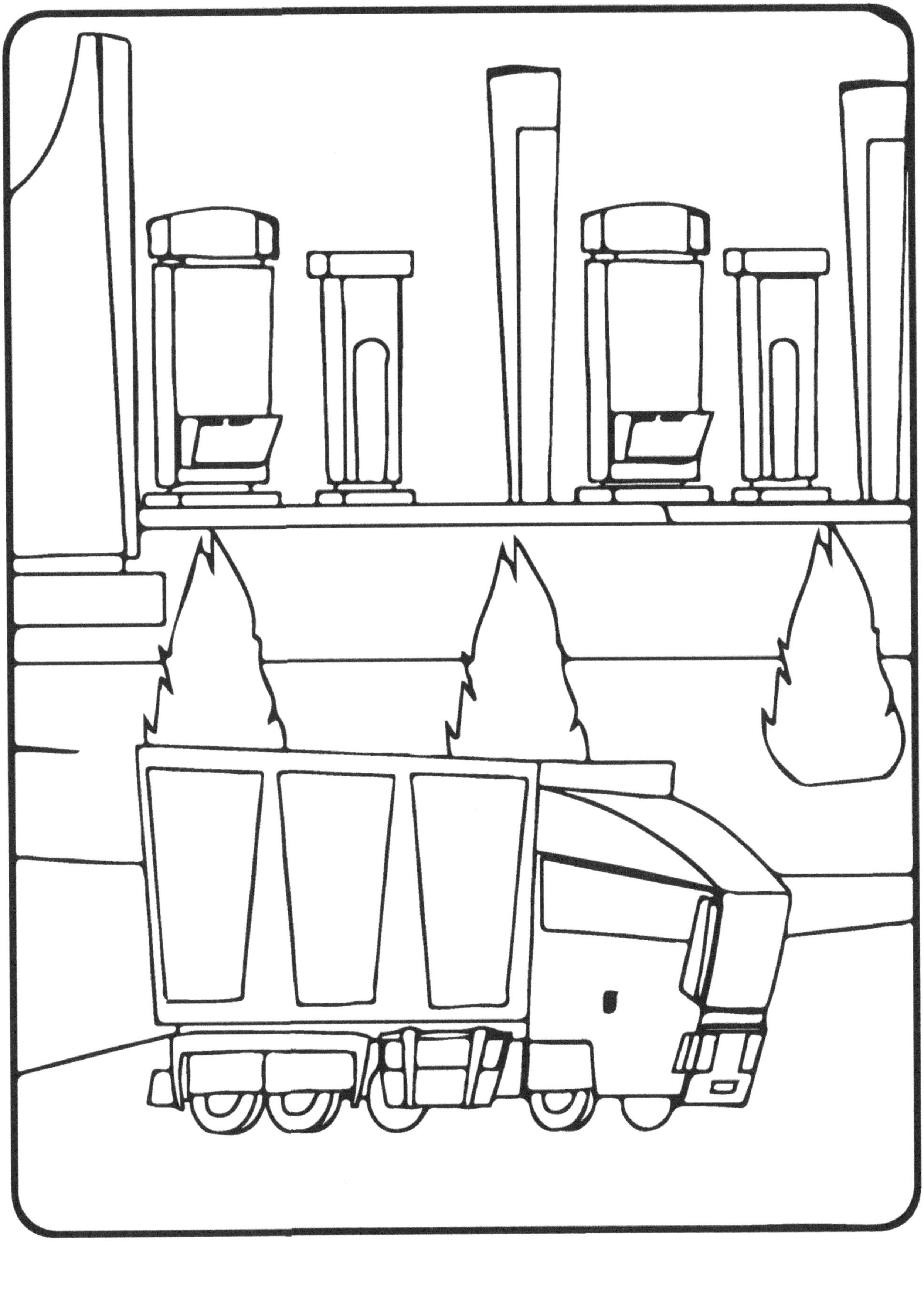

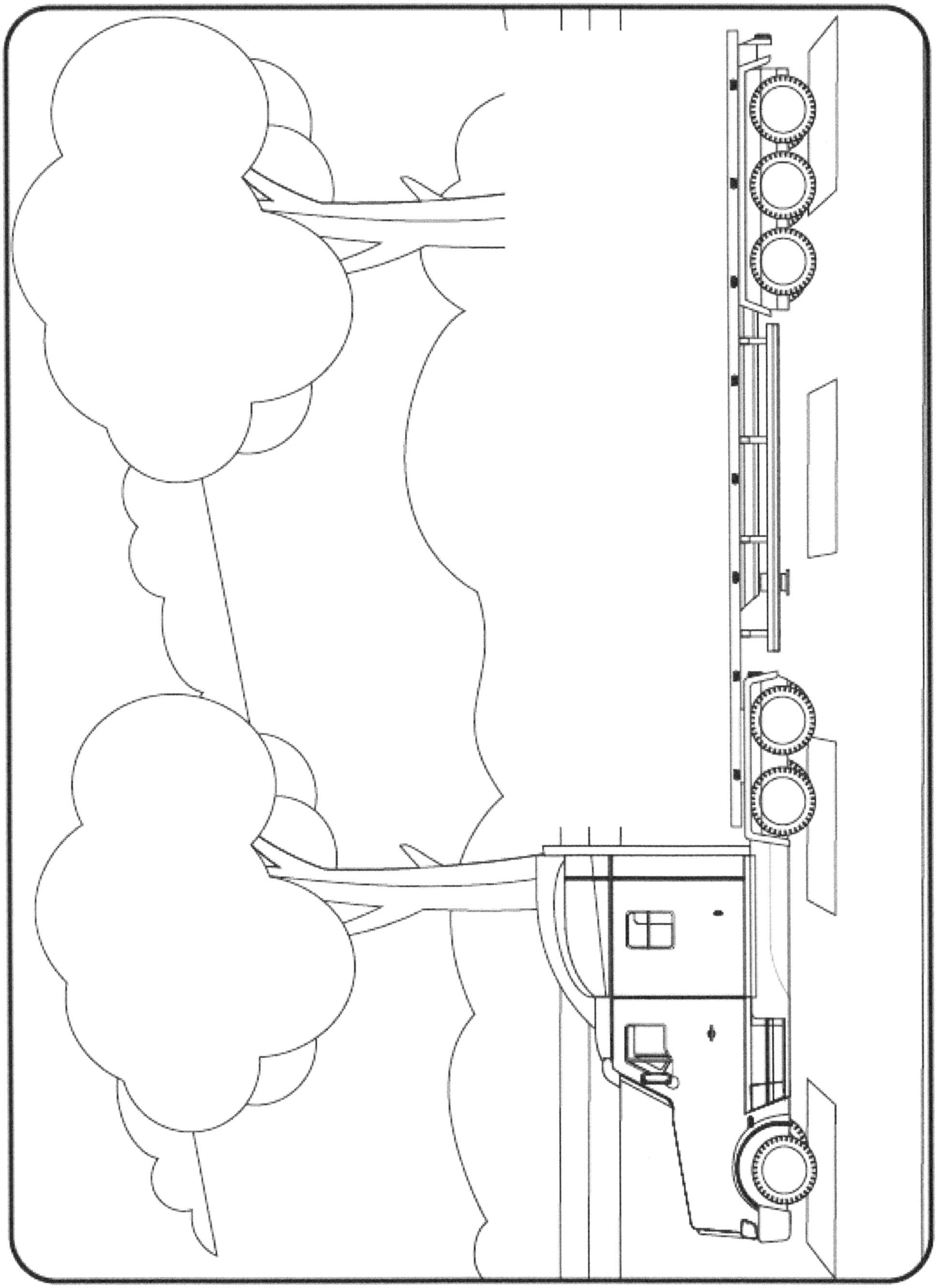

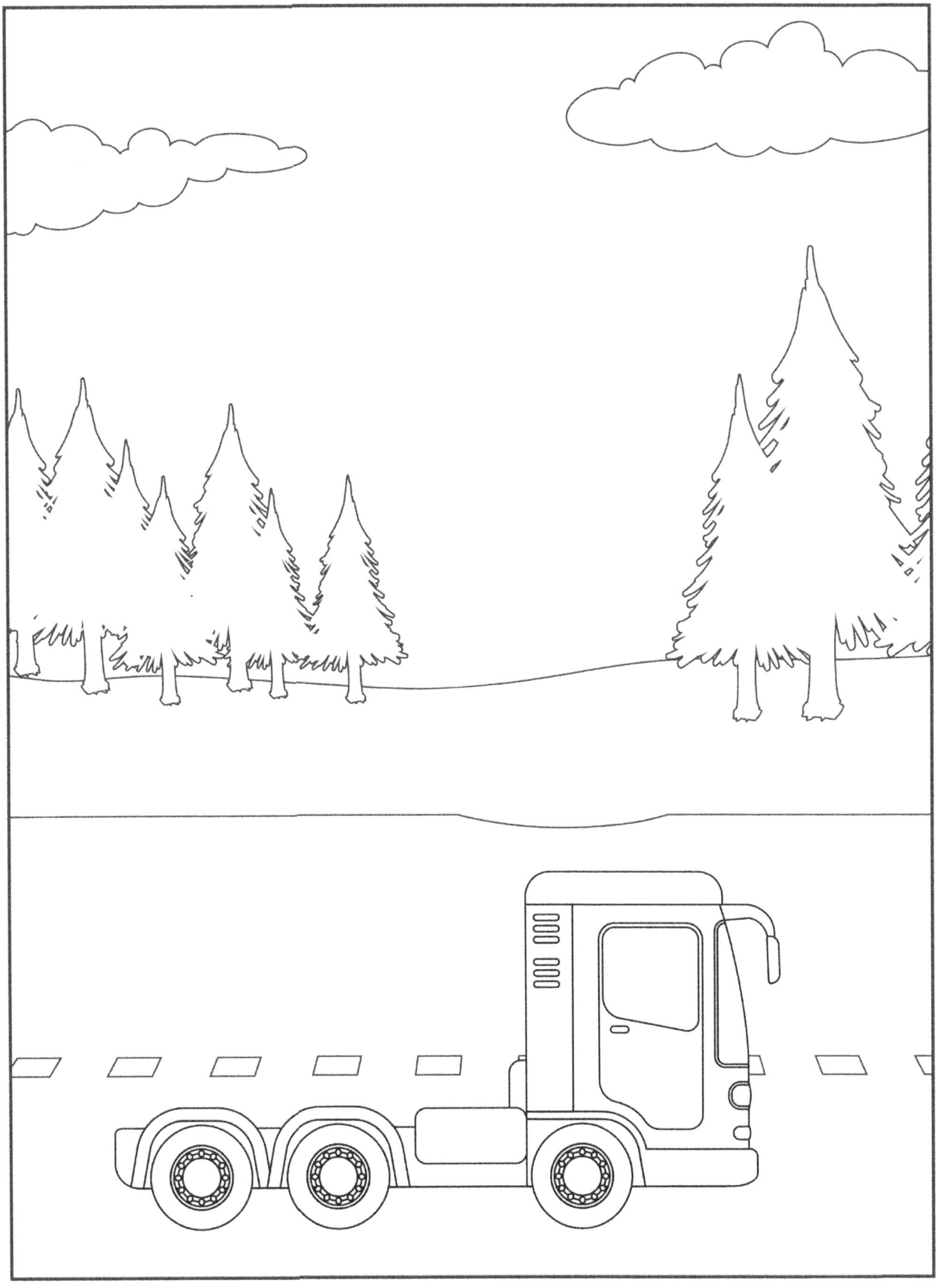

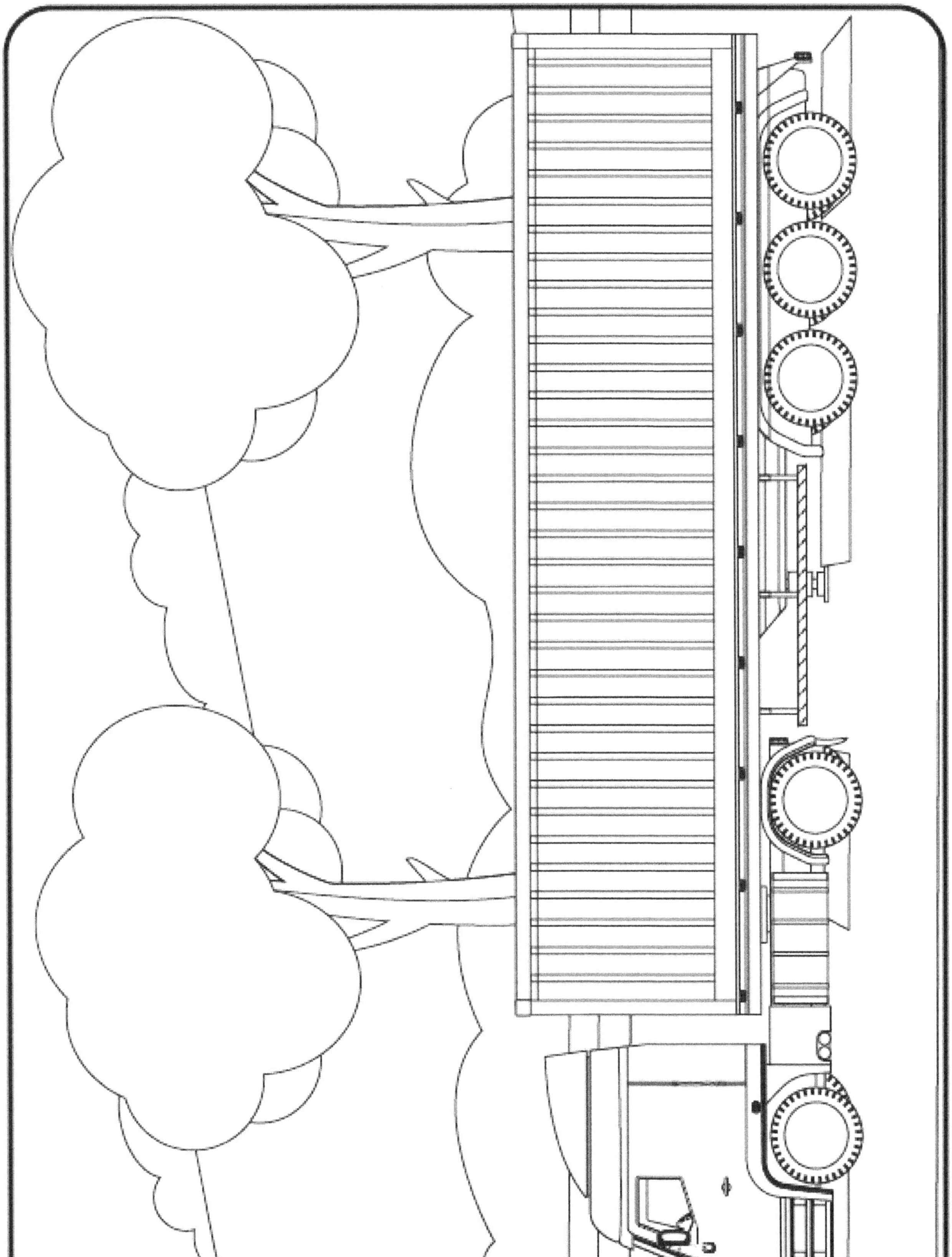

Imprint
Copyright Author:
Books4Moments
1st edition 2022

Contact: Markus Falb - Commercial Agency
Columbus street 7 / 4614 Marchtrenk /
Austria
UID No.: ATU76268389
E-Mail: office.falb@gmail.com

Made in the USA
Monee, IL
11 June 2022

97856820R10072